THE FIVE-MINUTE
HAIR
STYLIST

THE FIVE-MINUTE
HAIR
STYLIST

CHRISTINE MOODIE

Conceived and produced by Breslich & Foss, London

Photography by Gerald Wortman
Illustrations by Marilyn Leader
Text written in collaboration with Laura Wilson
Designed by Clare Finlaison
Original design by Lisa Tai

Quality production by Mandarin Offset Ltd, Hong Kong

Published by Crown Publishers, Inc., 201 East 50th Street
New York, New York 10022.
A member of the Crown Publishing Group.

CROWN is a trademark of Crown Publishers, Inc.

Manufactured in China

Library of Congress Cataloging-in-Publication Data

Moodie, Christine.
The five-minute hair stylist / Christine Moodie. — 1st ed.
p. cm.
1. Hairdressing 2. Braids (Hairdressing) I. Title.
TT972.M66 1991
646.7'245—dc20 90-2422
CIP

ISBN 0-517-58224-4

CONTENTS

THE FIVE MINUTE APPROACH

Your hair is one of the first things that people notice about you. A new hair style can make you feel great, which means you will look great as well. It can give a new look to an old outfit, or brighten you up when you're feeling low, and there is always that special occasion when you want to look your very best.

Magazines and beauty books tend to give general guidelines as to what will, and will not suit a particular bone structure — of course the shape of your face and head will make a difference to the way a style looks, but don't let yourself be pigeon-holed by this advice. Everyone is unique, and only by experimenting will you find the styles which are best for your looks. Your particular life-style will also make certain demands; speed and ease are usually among the most important. You may think it impossible to achieve some of the styles in this book in five hours, let alone five minutes but all it takes is practice. Take some time sitting in front of your mirror by yourself and experiment. If you are planning to wear a particular style for a special occasion, try it out first in the privacy of your bedroom or bathroom. Relax and enjoy yourself. Messing around with your hair can be great fun, and there is plenty of inspiration for new styles everywhere — on the street, on television, in films and magazines. A three-way mirror may be helpful in the beginning, but styling your own hair depends on touch, not sight. Your hands will soon learn the feel of your hair and you'll know what to do by instinct.

Always remember that the most elaborate hairstyle can be wrecked in the time it takes to pull a polo neck sweater over your head. Zippers can be hazardous, too — and quite painful if they get caught in the back hair. If in doubt, ask a friend to do you up at the back or dress yourself before styling your hair. Remember also that hats and scarves can flatten your hairstyle or pull it out of shape.

HAIR CARE

Washing: brush or comb your hair thoroughly before washing. Very hot water can be harmful to hair, so check that it is tepid or luke-warm. Wet your hair thoroughly under the shower head. Then put a small amount of shampoo into the palm of your hand and apply to the scalp, starting at the front hairline and working backwards. Rub the shampoo in with your fingertips, and squeeze it into the hair using your whole hand. Rinse your hair thoroughly before applying conditioner.

Harsh detergents can cause flakiness on the scalp. This can also be caused by a mild allergic reaction to shampoo, so choose with care. For dry or oily hair, choose an appropriate shampoo and conditioner.

1 *Barrettes or slides*
2 *Elastic ruffle*
3 *Covered elastic bands*
4 *Hairdresser's clip*
5 *Hairpins*
6 *Hairgrips*

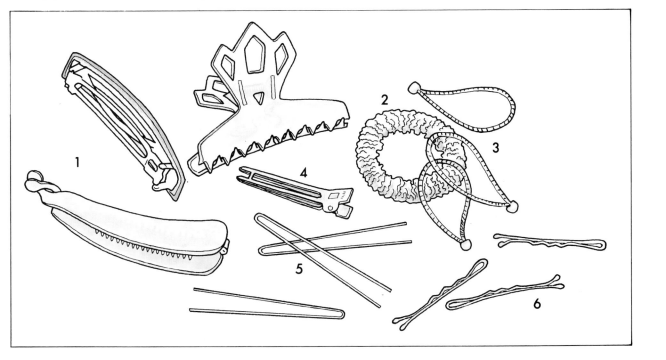

1 *Gather hair into a ponytail, but don't secure with a band.*

2 *Twist the ponytail all the way round twice, in a clockwise direction.*

3 *Holding the base of the ponytail firmly in one hand, lift up the end and fold down the top third towards the nape of the neck.*

4 *Fold the whole ponytail down under itself.*

5 *Cup the folded ponytail in* one hand, leaving a small space between it and the back of the head.

6 *Begin to push the upper portion of the ponytail over into the space with the other hand, so that the folded part is slowly rolling over into it.*

7 *When you have pushed all the hair in, secure with hairgrips along the seam formed by the join, starting at the bottom. Conceal the grips by pushing them right underneath the roll.*

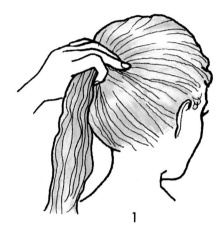

1

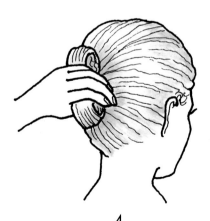

4

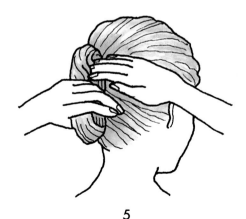

5

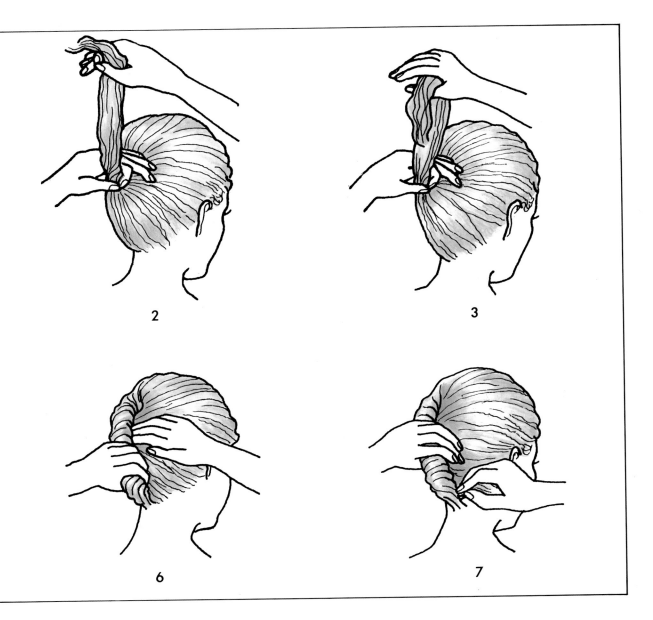

2

3

6

7

Conditioning: apply conditioner as you would a shampoo, and leave for 30 seconds to one minute before rinsing. Combing conditioner through your hair will ensure that it treats the ends as well as the roots.

Towel drying: drape the towel over your head and massage your scalp through the towel with the fingers and palms of your hands in a gentle circular motion until the hair is nearly dry. Rubbing vigorously between your palms may dry the hair faster, but it also rubs the hair the wrong way, which will weaken it and give it a dead, dull look.

Blow drying: always towel dry the hair first to remove excess water and allow time for natural drying before you start to blow dry. Repeated and prolonged blasts of very hot air can cause a dull, lifeless appearance, so don't hold the dryer close to one area of your head for too long and don't allow the scalp to get too hot.

Brushing: there are a variety of brushes available for different jobs. Shop around and see what suits you best. Bristles can be made of natural fibers, rubber or nylon. If you choose a nylon brush, make sure that the ends of the bristles are rounded to avoid scratching your scalp. Choose a round brush for a blow-dried style.

It used to be said that a hundred brush strokes before bedtime was a must for beautiful, shining hair. In fact, excess brushing creates friction, and may even damage the scalp. So try not to overdo it — it may be better to use a wide-toothed comb instead. Never, ever tug at your hair. Hair is a reasonably elastic fiber, but it will weaken, and may even break if subjected to too much yanking and stretching. Use a comb to tackle any really stubborn snarls or knots. Wait until your hair is dry, or almost dry, before brushing.

Brushes should be thoroughly cleaned at least once a week. If you neglect them, you'll be brushing dirt and grease right back into your hair. Soak them in tepid, soapy water, rinse well and leave them to dry naturally. Don't use dish washing detergent or harsh household soap, as this may cause an allergic reaction if it isn't properly rinsed.

Combing: combs, like brushes, come in a variety of materials — plastic being the most commonly used. However, rubber is often kinder to hair and less likely to scratch the skin. Use a comb with wide teeth on wet hair — if your hair is very tangled, try dampening it or using a little mousse to ease the knots. If you have long hair, keep a tail comb handy for those bouffant styles which need lifting. It will also be useful for shepherding stray locks back into place and easing knots loose.

Backcombing: backcombing is especially useful for bringing hair of different lengths into a manageable unit, or for a style which calls for a large volume of hair. Use a comb if you want stiffness or a brush for a looser effect. When you have finished backcombing, smooth over the top hair in the direction you want it to lie.

Scrunch Drying: this is a good way to ensure that your hair has plenty of lift and body when it is dry. Use a dryer, and bring your hand up underneath your hair, squeezing it with a gentle crushing motion (like crushing a piece of paper). For straight or wavy hair, squirt a little mousse into the palm of your hand and scrunch it into your hair.

PRODUCTS AND EQUIPMENT
Curling iron: the heat generated by a curling iron is very intense, so it is vital to bend the hair at the right angle, or you will be left with a series of strange-looking ridges and no curls.

1 *Take a small section of hair and twist between finger and thumb before winding in a shaper.*

2 *Roll the hair around the shaper, turning it through 360 degrees each time.*

3 *Roll the shaper right up to the roots of the hair and secure tightly.*

4 *Unwind gently and allow your hair to cool before styling.*

Curling the hair well round the tongs of the iron before closing them also helps to prevent this effect. Be careful when using the curling iron near your face, as it is easy to burn yourself.

Shapers: these can be heated or unheated. If you want your hair to curl, take a small amount of hair per shaper, as the heat must be able to penetrate right through the hair. In any case, the heat will penetrate better if you roll the hair along its length, not just in the middle. For waves, use larger sections of hair.

When you roll up the hair in the shaper, remember to keep it at an angle from your head, upwards and outwards, never straight down. Angle the front hair straight up. To make sure they stay in place, twist the ends into an 'S' shape.

The longer you leave the shaper in, the curlier your hair will be, but don't leave them for more than 15 minutes if they are heated. You can give them an extra twist once they are in to ensure that they stay firm. You can wash the shapers in a mild detergent after use.

Gel: a jelly-like substance used for setting the hair after shampooing. As the hair dries, so the gel dries and hardens, holding the hair in shape until it is dampened or washed again. Apply by squeezing gel into the palm of your hand and use the tips of your fingers to work the hair into the desired shape.

If you want to re-apply gel to revive a flagging hairstyle, be sure to brush out any old gel first, because 'dead' gel tends to form into flakes, which can look like dandruff.

Mousse: this is also for setting hair, but unlike gel, you can scrunch mousse into your hair as you blow dry. It does not give as firm a hold as gel, but it doesn't flake out of your hair and look unsightly, either.

Hairspray: traditionally used in conjunction with plenty of backcombing for the construction of enormous beehives, hairspray has had rather a bad press recently for damaging hair

1 *Take a section of hair from across the top of the head.*

2 *Divide into three equal sections.*

3 *Braid the first two turns in the normal way — right strand over center strand, left over right, center over left etc.*

4 *Take up a strand of loose hair from the side of the head and add it to the strand you are braiding.*

5 *Continue to take up loose hair and weave into braid, taking alternatively from each side.*

6 *Merge the newest strand with the oldest as you go.*

7 *Once you have woven all the loose hair into the braid, braid normally and secure the end with a band.*

1

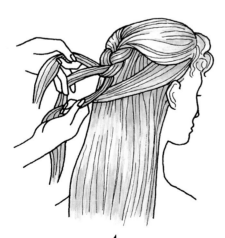

4

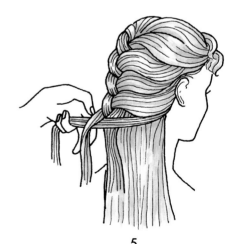

5

2

3

6

7

(it works by glueing the hair shafts together to form a mat of hair) and the environment (it makes a hole in the ozone layer).

Nevertheless, it remains the best way of securing an elaborate style or shaping a simple one. Choose an ozone friendly brand, and be sure to brush all the spray out before you go to bed. Hold the spray can nine to twelve inches away from your hair to ensure even coverage, keeping the spray well away from your eyes and mouth.

Hair wax: this is especially good for finishing your hairstyle, smoothing and putting stray locks or individual curls in place. Take a small amount of wax, rub it between your fingers, apply to the hair between fingers and thumb.

Hairgrips: these are used to hold the hair in place. They are the cement in the structure of the style.

Hairpins: these are used to tuck in stray pieces of hair, and for any tidying up that needs to be done once a style is in place. They are far more easily concealed than grips, and will not damage the shape if pushed in with care.

BASIC HAIR TYPES

Dry hair: frequent washing (every two to three days) is essential for dry hair. Use a very mild shampoo and plenty of conditioner. If you can bear it, a final rinse in cold water is a good way of stimulating the scalp. Allow your hair to dry naturally as often as possible. Always rub gently with a towel before using the hairdryer. Try not to use tongs or heated rollers unless you absolutely have to as these tend to exacerbate the condition. To achieve more volume, or a curly effect, dry with fingers or use shapers overnight. Have your hair trimmed regularly to prevent split ends. If your scalp is very dry, massage it regularly with a few drops of a natural oil, such as almond or walnut.

Oily hair: as with dry hair, wash regularly using a gentle shampoo. When washing, don't attack your scalp too vigorously. Oily hair is caused by over enthusiastic sebacious glands, so don't stimulate them more than you need. Similarly, try not to brush it too much since every time you brush, you are encouraging the sebum. Use a comb or a brush with soft bristles instead.

If your hair is fine, then a shorter style may be preferable. There are plenty of dry shampoos on the market which save the trouble of daily washing, but resist the temptation to use them on a regular basis as they tend to clog the roots of the hair. Never, ever, dredge your hair with talcum powder, even if you feel desperate.

Use lemon juice or vinegar in your rinse water as a natural method of combatting oily hair.

Normal hair: you are lucky. But remember, your hair will only stay well behaved if you treat it with respect. Badly rinsed hair will have a dull appearance no matter how healthy it is, and it could result in a dry scalp. Use a good shampoo with plenty of conditioner to keep the shine.

Mixed condition: like the skin on the face, hair can be oily in some places and dry in others. The most common combination is hair which is oily at the roots and dry at the ends. Use a mild shampoo and apply conditioner to the ends of the hair only. Blow-dry very gently, and avoid using a curling iron, heated rollers or shapers excessively.

SOME PROBLEMS
Dandruff: it is easy to mistake a dry, flaky scalp for dandruff. A dry scalp which is neglected can turn into dandruff, and scratching an itchy scalp may make it infected. Dandruff is caused by a faster than normal skin cell growth, and from either

too much or too little sebum being produced. There are specialist dandruff shampoos on the market, but if you find that large, loose flakes of skin are detaching themselves and your head feels constantly itchy, you should see a doctor.

Allergies: over-use of harsh shampoos, bleaching, coloring or perming lotions can all cause itching and rashes. If you know that your skin is sensitive, it's best to try a 'patch test' on your arm or leg before applying something to your head. It could be that you need to see a dermatologist for a specially formulated shampoo or cleanser. In any case, try not to get shampoo on your face and never bleach or color your hair without wearing rubber gloves and protecting your face and clothing.

Hair loss: Alopecia, or baldness, is a medically recognized condition. If you suffer from persistent hair loss, it is best to consult a doctor. Mild hair loss can be caused by poor diet, over-coloring, or bleaching. Bleaches contain a combination of ammonia and hydrogen peroxide which is very harmful to the roots of the hair. Hair which is both permed and bleached is particularly susceptible.

HAIRDRESSERS
Many people feel overawed by hairdressers, especially if they operate in fashionable and expensive surroundings. It is easy to let yourself be persuaded into having a cut or style that you don't actually want, which is why it is best to have a firm idea of what you *do* want before you step inside. Find a hairdresser you can trust, and stick to them. If your style needs regular cutting, perming or coloring, then a regular hairdresser will get to know your requirements and keep a note of which shade or bleach to use, which saves a lot of time and trouble all round.

Remember that some styles need a lot of maintenance such as setting in rollers, or complicated blow-drying techniques. If you feel you can't cope with the style, say so. After all, it's your hair.

1
AT HOME

SIMPLE TWISTS

What you need
Hair grips
Ornament, barrette or
  slide

Hair Type
Medium – Long
Straight, Wavy, Curly

This is an easy and attractive way of keeping long hair from flopping across your face and getting in your eyes. Twisting the hair as you take it back from your face gives a well groomed look to an otherwise casual style. The natural looseness at the back balances it perfectly, making the most of clean, shining hair.

It is vital to brush your hair thoroughly before you start. Separate it carefully to ensure that the same amount of hair is taken back on each side, otherwise you will have a tension problem. This is important, as nothing looks worse than a hairstyle which is floppy on one side and painfully tight on the other. The hair should be drawn back smoothly, in a single movement, so that it looks like one whole strand. Thick, curly hair is especially prone to lumps and bumps, although the cascade of curls down your back will look stunning. Straight hair will give a well defined twist and a sleeker, more streamlined look to this style.

1 *Take a section of hair from temple to above ear and separate, using comb.*

2 *Begin to twist hair towards head until quite tight. Secure at the back.*

3 *Repeat the process on the other side.*

4 *Pin an ornament over the joined sections. Check that hairgrips are concealed.*

QUICK QUIFF

What you need
Hair pins
Hair grips
Covered elastic band
Ornament

Hair Type
Medium – Long
Straight, Wavy, Curly

This is an updated version of the quiff which has a nostalgic Forties feel. It can be casual or sophisticated, soft or severe, depending on how tightly the hair is pulled back from the face. For a way of converting this casual style into a more formal look, see the following page.

It is an excellent style for hair which is layered in front. It is also ideal for anyone who is 'growing out' bangs or a fringe, as all the infuriating loose ends can be tucked in and forgotten. If you have shorter hair, the quiff can be worn on its own, with the hair loose at the back. The ponytail provides a more balanced look for longer hair. Even if you do not intend to wear a ponytail as part of the finished style, it is a useful means of keeping the back hair out the way while you attend to the front. Keep a couple of hair pins handy to push any stray hair back into the quiff.

1 Divide off front hair, about 1½" above the ears by parting horizontally across head. Tie remaining hair in band.

2 Lift front hair, pushing slightly forward and twisting.

3 Insert finger underneath roll of hair and pin quiff from the back.

4 Make sure all pins are concealed beneath ornament.

Quick quiff variation

Simply turning your ponytail into a little roll gives this style a smart appearance, whether it is worn with a business suit or a sweater and draped scarf, like the one shown here. The roll at the back balances the quiff perfectly. This hairstyle looks superb from all angles; the structure of the quiff at the back and sides is as pleasing as the front (see previous page for original style).

Keep the roll low on the head: it should be as near the nape of the neck as possible. If the roll is placed too high, the head is made to look a rather strange shape, especially if the back of your head is quite flat. It is important to ensure that any shorter ends are tucked into the hair, or you could be left with hair whizzing out in all directions.

If your hairline is low at the back, there may be some little fuzzy hairs which can't be incorporated into the roll. Try smoothing them into the hair with wax.

1 *Remove any ornament from the ponytail, but retain the band. Twist the hair, making sure any loose ends are tucked in.*

2 *Bring the hair up and around, pinning it underneath.*

Plaid ponytail

What you need
2 covered elastic bands
Length of ribbon
(width 1″–1½″)

Hair Type
Medium – Long
Straight, Wavy, Curly

This is a new look for the traditional ponytail. An ideal style for sports — the hair is kept well away from the face and the back of the neck. This ponytail doesn't need to be augmented with headbands (which slip) or hair pins (which fly off in all directions). Choose a ribbon which matches your tennis shirt or leotard or one which provides a colorful contrast to an all-white sports outfit. Two ribbons in contrasting colors may be used, providing they are the same length. Tie them together before you start.

Smooth the ponytail firmly with your hands to prevent any bulges forming as you wrap your ribbon. If your hair is layered at the back, wrap the ribbon tightly and make sure that there are no gaps at the sides where the shorter ends can escape. Drawing the hair back firmly at the nape of the neck will stop hair from falling out at the top of the ponytail.

1 *Secure hair at nape of neck with band. Smooth ponytail with hands and secure again at the bottom.*

2 *Tie length of ribbon at the top of the ponytail and make a small bow.*

3 *Bind the ribbon round the ponytail crossing at the back and front alternately. Make a small bow at the bottom.*

BEAUTIFUL BRAIDS

What you need
2 covered elastic bands
Ribbon or ornament

Hair type
Medium – Long
Straight, Wavy, Curly

This style has an easy, natural charm. It looks best with squeaky clean hair and just a hint of make-up. Blonde or light auburn hair looks especially lovely when braided, as the individual strands show up well and the many different shades in natural fair hair give a beautiful sunny look.

Two braids are easier to manage than one, as the volume of hair is not so great. (See page 14 for basic technique). Once you have divided the hair, keep the sections separate to avoid a messy 'thatched' effect at the back of your head. However, it is best not to part the hair too severely at the back or pull the braids too tightly. Keep a fairly long switch of hair at the bottom of the braid.

Straight hair tends to be easier to braid than curly hair, simply because it is easier to control. However, escaping wisps of straight hair give a braid a rather ragged appearance, whereas escaping curls have a nice soft effect.

1 *Divide hair loosely at nape of neck.*

2 *Braid each section from just above the nape. Secure each braid separately with a band.*

3 *Remove both bands and tie braids together using only one. Add ribbon or ornament of your choice.*

Short shapes

What you need
Hair gel

Hair type
Short
Straight, Wavy

Short hair requires frequent attention from a hairdresser, although any well cut style will keep its basic shape as it grows. However, a week before your regular haircut, you may begin to feel that your hair is unmanageable and messy. Play up the mess with this style, and create a new look. It can look gamine with your leather jacket and jeans, accessorized with big hoop earrings or shades. It won't go flat if you want to wear a beret or headscarf if you shake your head and fluff up your hair when you take off your headgear. For an instant evening look, apply red lipstick and bold eye make-up. The pointed fringe or bangs creates a dramatic effect, but it can be left to fall naturally if you prefer a softer shape.

Gelling and lifting the hair in this way gives it a lot of movement — you can run your hands through it as often as you like. If you are using a lot of gel, be sure to brush out before re-styling. Wash your hair every few days to keep it looking shiny and fresh.

1 Apply a generous amount of gel to hair.

2 Comb hair forward from the crown and above the ears. Smooth back hair down towards nape of neck.

3 Starting at the crown begin to lift hair with fingers all around the head, keeping it in the same direction.

4 Form fringe or bangs into points with fingers.

WRAPPED PONYTAIL

What you need
Covered elastic band
Hair grips
Hair wax

Hair type
Medium – Long
Straight, Wavy, Curly

A brilliant way of converting an ordinary ponytail into something special, this style is especially good if you are entertaining at home and expect the guest at any moment. All you need to do is separate out some hair at each side of your ponytail, wrap it around, and pin. Add your favorite shirt, best earrings and a squirt of perfume. If you intended to wash your hair but didn't have time, the style may work even better. Although freshly clean hair feels great, slightly dirty hair is often easier to manage.

As this style has to be done completely 'blind', using hair wax will make the strands you are going to wrap easier to control. Take a little wax on your fingertips and rub them together. Then smooth the strands with it to stop any wisps of hair falling out of place. Keep the wax handy in case the hair starts to unwrap itself.

In order to create this style, you really need to have hair which is all one length. Wrapping the ponytail in hair of different lengths is almost impossible, as the shorter bits will stick out and look very odd. As with the Simple Twists (see page 22), the wrap will be more clearly defined with straight hair.

1 *Make a ponytail at the nape of the neck, securing with a covered elastic band.*

2 *Take two small section of hair from each side of the ponytail.*

3 *Twist sections around the ponytail one at a time in opposite directions, making sure the band is covered. Secure with hairgrips.*

SIMPLE BRAID

What you need
2 hair combs
Hair grips
Covered elastic
Ornament or ribbon

Hair type
Medium – Long
Straight, Wavy, Curly

A beautiful braid displays both the beauty of your hair and your flair as a hairdresser to their best advantage with the minimum of effort. It looks intricate, but braiding is a simple skill, and, once your hands learn what to do, it is very quick. Braids are practical as well as attractive. Once secured, your hair will remain in place — even in a howling gale — and you won't have to give it another thought.

This style is endlessly versatile. You can decorate it to suit your mood, braiding in a ribbon or a lightweight scarf. You can even stuff it under a hat without damaging it.

It is vital to brush your hair thoroughly before you start, and to divide the sections firmly with a comb. Make sure you keep hold of all three strands while braiding, by passing them from hand to hand. If any pieces of hair escape, poke them in again with a tail comb and fix with spray.

1 Draw back a section of hair from each side of the face, lift and twist slightly. Secure with a comb.

2 Divide hair into three sections and braid, leaving a fairly long tassel of unbraided hair at the end.

3 Bring the braid over your shoulder, secure with covered elastic and fix ornament. Tuck stalks under band.

4 Curl loose hair around the face by rolling tightly around your forefinger, holding for a second to make a loose curl.

ALPINE BRAIDS

What you need
2 covered elastic bands
Hair pins
Hair grips

Hair type
Long
Straight, Wavy, Curly

Traditional in many European countries, this hairstyle has a strong flavor of Heidi, goats with bells and dirndl skirts, but it is popular with women of all ages. Perfect for windy days, walking the dog, or hiking — this style has a pretty, practical country feel. It is ideal for winter sports, as the braids fit neatly under a woolly ski hat. For the evening, you could try a gypsy look with gold hoop earrings and a boldly figured shawl over bare shoulders.

   Make a fairly loose parting so that the hair is not pulled too tightly at the back. Starting the braids slightly above the nape will help keep a firm shape. If your hair is not quite long enough for the braids to join at the top of your head, discreet pins or a small barrette will cover the gap. It isn't necessary to have bangs or a fringe of course, but this will also prevent a gap from showing. Flowers or ornaments can be secured behind the braids, using long pins.

1 *Part hair, braid on each side and secure with bands.*

2 *Cross the braids at the back of the neck and bring them forwards over the shoulders.*

3 *Remove bands from braids and braid each as far as possible. Pin at the top. Pin the sides where necessary.*

Upside down bob

What you need
Water spray
Hair gel
Hair dryer

Hair Type
Short
Wavy, Curly

This soft, feminine bob frames the face beautifully and looks smart with anything. It is a style with a lot of movement; you can muss it up as much as you like. A side part looks best, but try to use your natural part, or the hair may escape and flop over your face.

The best time to style this bob is when you have just washed your hair. If your hair is dry, you can use a water spray to dampen it. These can be bought from any store selling household items. If you have curly, dry hair which tends to go into an uncontrollable frizz, spraying with water is an efficient way of keeping it manageable while you're styling it.

Use a wide-toothed comb to arrange your bob into the shape you want. If you have straight hair, use heated shapers to get curls, and then gel your hair and lift from the roots to create the same effect. Don't dampen the hair or you'll lose the curls. If you feel that the hair is going flat, push your fingers through it, lifting slightly as you go. You can fluff up the hair at the sides to keep the shape.

1 *Dampen hair slightly and apply gel to roots.*

2 *Dry hair upside down, scrunching with fingers.*

3 *Shake head and arrange hair using fingers and/or a comb.*

2
IN THE
CITY

FRENCH BRAID

What you need
Covered elastic band
Ribbon

Hair type
Medium – Long
Straight, Wavy

This style may look impossible but with a little practice, this complicated braid can be accomplished in seconds rather than minutes. Once you have mastered the technique of French, or inverted, braiding, an endless number of variations are possible. This style works best on straight hair, wavy hair or fine curls. Very thick curly hair tends to give a bumpy appearance on the top of the head.

Check that you have equal tension on both sides of the braid, or you will end up with one side tight and the other side loose and floppy. You can adjust the tension with your fingers or a tailcomb as you go, but be careful not to drop the three sections of the braid. Most people find it easiest to hold them in between two fingers.

Excellent for work because it is neat and extremely secure, this style can easily be transformed; (see the following page). Although the beautiful crossover effect of this style does not really need further decoration, it is possible to fix a row of small flowers or buds in between the braided strands. Once you get very efficient at braiding, you could work in colored ribbon down the center.

1 *Divide hair into sections (see page 14 for basic braid instructions).*

2 *Start to braid at the top of the head.*

3 *Complete braid and secure with band.*

FRENCH BRAID VARIATION

What you need
Covered elastic band
Ribbon or ornament

Hair type
Medium – Long
Straight, Wavy

Putting your hair up usually involves taking it through at least one other style on the way. This is one way of altering the French Braid on the previous page to give the hairstyle a more formal, finished look. At the same time, this 'half-up, half-down' style is also practical hiking or riding (a horse or a motorcycle). It stays secure in the wind and can be tucked under a scarf, a helmet or a hard hat. It looks good with a trilby or a panama, too.

Braid your hair as far down as you can possibly go to minimize the risk of escaping ends. As you tuck the braid under, keep a firm hand over the end so that the smaller turns don't come loose. Stretch the band first with your fingers so that it goes right over both parts of the braid.

1 Remove band and continue braiding to the bottom.

2 Tuck the end of the braid up and secure both parts together with a band. Add ribbon or ornament of your choice.

Classic bob

What you need
Mousse

Hair Type
Short
Straight, Wavy

The bob was the height of fashion in the 1920s when hemlines and hairlines suddenly shot up, and it has been popular ever since. In those days, bobbing your hair was thought to be an act of rebellion. Debates about it raged in the newspapers for weeks. F. Scott Fitzgerald even wrote a short story about it. These days, a well cut bob is the epitome of chic. As with all shorter cuts, the basic shape is very important.

The style can be carefree and casual or more disciplined and business-like; it goes equally well with a baggy sweater or a tailored suit. It is easy to control: a well cut bob can be washed, styled and forgotten. If you want more height on the top of the head, simply lift the hair from the roots with your fingers. If your hair is completely straight, use some heated shapers for a loose, gentle wave. A fringe or bangs can be finger waved with the help of a little wax, or, if your hair remains stubbornly straight, use a curling iron first.

1 Comb in mousse on the top of the hair.

2 Fluff out hair at the sides by scrunching with a little mousse.

BRAIDED CHIGNON

What you need
2 covered elastic bands
Hair grips

Hair type
Medium – Long
Straight, Wavy

It isn't necessary to sacrifice your crowning glory in order to conquer Wall Street or the City. With this type of style, long hair can look just as business-like as short hair. This is just one of the variations on the French braid shown on page 44. Again, it is more effective with straight hair.

Allow your hair to fall into its natural part. If it is a side part, this will mean that one braid will be considerably thicker than the other. However, this will not look peculiar, as the two braids join together as one at the back of the head. In fact, a side part seems to fit the style better.

This basic shape, favored by a whole generation of cinema heroines in the 1940s — very Lauren Bacall, cool, capable and strong — is completely appropriate for the business woman of today.

1 *Braid both sides to the nape of the neck. Secure with bands (see page 14 for basic braid instructions).*

2 *Remove bands, taking care to keep the two ends separate.*

3 *Divide the two ends into three strands for braiding. Braid together in the normal way.*

4 *Secure end with elastic, tuck under and pin into place.*

SIMPLE BRAID VARIATION

What you need
Covered elastic band
Hair pins

Hair type
Medium – Long
Straight, Wavy, Curly

If you feel that your long braid needs to look a little more formal, or you feel like a change, it is simple to turn it into a full-blown hair-do. You just turn it up and pin in to position. With this hairstyle, you already have two beautiful combs for decoration — anything more would be superfluous (see page 36).

Make sure that the combs stay in place throughout or the hair will sag downwards at the sides. If they slip once the braid is tucked under and pinned, it will be impossible to save the side hair, and you will have to start again.

Push the pins well into the hair. This braid is very solid, and pins have to grip firmly or they will slide out and you will find a row of pin ends protruding from either side of the braid. If you don't feel confident about the pins, check them by running a finger down the sides of the braid from time to time.

1 Remove the band and continue braiding to the end. Lift the braid up and tuck the end in underneath.

2 Secure with pins along each side of the braid.

Cavalier bow

What you need
Hair pins
Covered elastic band
Ribbon or scarf

Hair type
Long
Straight, Wavy, Curly

This is a good way of controlling very long, thick hair at work while keeping a fall of heavy curls, ringlets or a thick glossy swathe of straight hair looking wonderful. This style with its big bold bow has a dashing, gallant feel to it, almost swashbuckling; it gives a dark, formal business suit a special touch of individuality.

You can make a bow like this one out of stiff, wide ribbon and attach it to a hair pin. If you are worried that the ribbon will slip and the band will show, wrap a small piece of the same colored ribbon around the band and pin your bow to this. Alternatively, you can buy ready-made bows attached to hair slides or barrettes which hold the ponytail securely. For a different effect, try a chiffon or silk scarf. Make the bow as large and flamboyant as you like, in strong, plain colors. A small bow or a nondescript pattern will look insignificant and minimize the impact of this dramatic style.

1 *Roll hair from just above the ears. You can do both sides together.*

2 *Join the rolls at the back with pins.*

3 *Secure hair with an elastic at the nape of the neck. Add ribbon of your choice.*

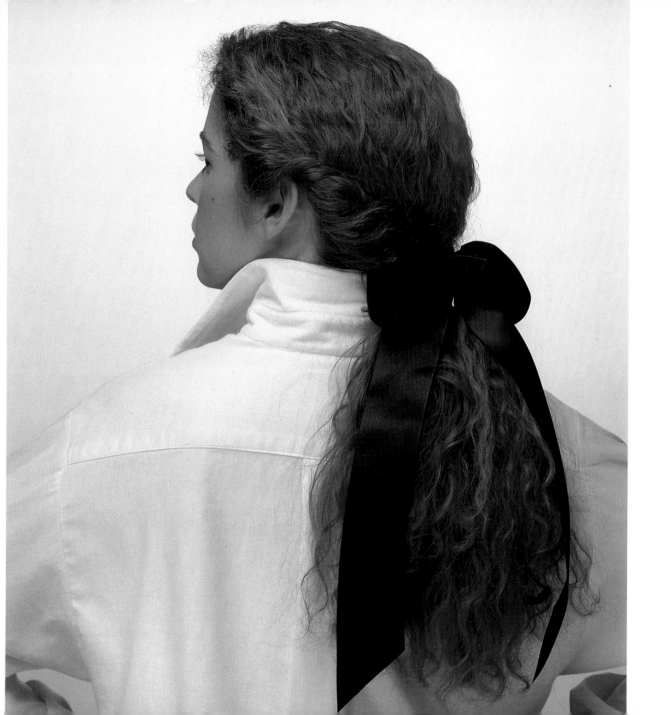

SIMPLE CHIGNON

What you need
Covered elastic band
Hair pins
Ribbon or ornament

Hair type
Medium
Straight, Wavy, Curly

This is a neat, reliable style, and the elegant curves of hair look especially good in profile. It is ideally suited to medium length hair. If your hair is much more than shoulder length, it becomes too much to tuck in neatly, and too heavy to stay there without an armory of pins. The base of the ponytail needs to be reasonably high on the head, otherwise there will not be enough room to form the chignon. Tuck the ponytail under securely, so that it doesn't become loose and start to poke through the top layer of hair.

Choose a blouse or sweater with a simple neck — a high, fussy collar will interfere with the way the hair falls and give a cluttered look. This style can be decorated with a ribbon or light-weight scarf. For a less formal look, tuck a few flowers into the band (short stems will be hidden in the bulk of hair). For an evening make-over, see page 82.

1 Make a ponytail in the middle of the back of your head. Secure with band.

2 Grasp ponytail half way down, tucking hair under. Comb the hair inwards around your hand.

3 Tuck the hair right under and pin. Add ribbon or ornament.

4 Attach top sides of hair with pin. The pin should be concealed by the ribbon or ornament.

FRENCH ROLL

What you need
Hair grips

Hair type
Medium – Long
Straight, Wavy

This timeless classic is simply the most elegant of shapes and the best of taste. Understated and utterly stylish, this glossy roll of hair needs no decoration. It is suitable for any occasion: a day at work, a night at the opera, whatever you like. Stick to classic accessories: pearls, your best silk scarf, delicate earrings. Loud colors and fake 'fun' jewelry do not belong here. However, if you want to make the roll a little more frivolous, turn to page 86 for a quick party conversion.

The construction of this style is the most important thing (see page 8 for basic method). After you have wrapped your hair around your hand, be sure to withdraw it very carefully so that you don't ruin the shape. If the hair has been well brushed and wrapped around cleanly, this will be much easier. You may have some difficulty concealing all the pins. A well-made Fench roll will look seamless, with the pins pushed well into the hair. You will be able to feel if the pins are working loose and you can just push them in with your fingers.

1 *Draw all your hair to the back of your head and wrap around one hand.*

2 *Withdraw your hand and hold the rolled hair in place.*

3 *Beginning at the middle 'seam' of the hair, secure with pins. Tuck in the hair at the nape of the neck.*

4 *Form the top of the roll into a neat coil and secure.*

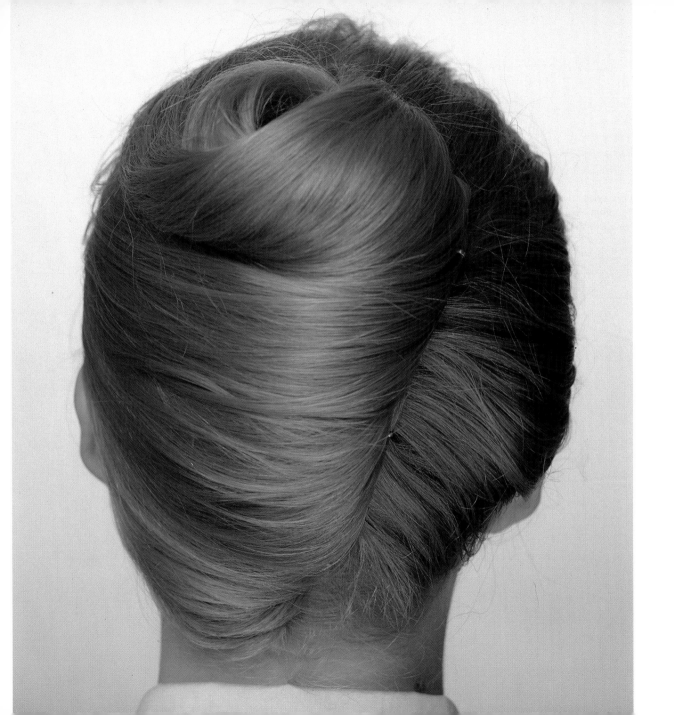

DOUBLE PONYTAIL

This is a high security ponytail for unruly hair. A large volume of hair can look wonderful, but its heavy weight means that it will not be restrained for long by an ordinary ponytail. Your hair may be well behaved at the beginning of the day, but constant fall-out means that you either have to push it back every few seconds or end up looking like a cave woman. The ornament on the back of the head avoids hair coming loose from the bunch; it is especially useful if your hair is slightly shorter at the front.

You can make an elastic ruffle for yourself, using a scrap of material. A stiff fabric, either plain or bold patterned, such as brocade or velvet will work best. This one is made from organza. Try experimenting with different types of hair ornaments in contrasting colors and textures for a series of different looks.

Check that the hair is symmetrical: the top hair should join in the middle of the back of the head and the ponytail must align with it. Measure the amount of hair you take from the front with your eye. Equal amounts on both sides will ensure that the style doesn't look lopsided.

1 *Take sections of hair from each side of the head above the ears and bring together at the crown. Smooth with comb.*

2 *Insert barrettes to secure the two sections of hair.*

3 *Bring all hair together and secure with elastic ruffle.*

3
NIGHT AND
DAY

SLEEK CHIC

What you need
Hair gel
Chopstick or tail comb

Hair type
Short
Straight, Wavy

This style leaves your face very bare, so the overall effect will depend on the shape of your face and style of make-up. You could opt for the androgynous look, or use bold, dark eye make-up and pillar box red lipstick for a *femme fatale* effect. For a really radical, striking look, use a light colored matt foundation and a strong lipstick, but leave your eyes completely natural. You can stop at the first step and leave the hair plastered down flat. If your hair begins to fall forward, simply add more gel using the palms of your hands.

A chopstick is the ideal implement for lifting your hair, because of its shape and length. If you don't have one handy, use a tail comb. Make sure that no trace of a parting remains, or your hair will tend to fall sideways, instead of straight back.

However you do this style, it requires a great deal of gel, so always wash it out afterwards. You may find that an extra application of shampoo is necessary.

1 *Gel hair all over, slicking the hair back.*

2 *Loosen and lift with a chopstick.*

LOVE KNOT

Straight out of a pre-Raphaelite painting, this free, floating style has a lyrical feel. Medieval angels and fairy tale princesses wear their hair like this. This loose knot on the top of your head can be achieved with very few pins, and it doesn't matter if wisps of hair escape — that is all part of its charm.

Choose loose clothes in silk or wool; soft folds and unstructured garments suit this style best. Keep jewelry to an absolute minimum, and pin on a flower instead. Any small, firm flower such as a rose bud or carnation can be attached to the hair with long pins.

If your hair is straight, use heated shapers to make ringlets. It is best to make them quite tight at first, as the weight of hair will loosen the curl considerably during the course of an evening. If you want a few wisps of hair in front of the ears, curl them round your fingers. Short thin strands of hair near the face are difficult to curl with a curling iron, and it is surprisingly easy to burn your cheek.

1 *Take a section of hair from above the ear, bring it up and twist round, pivoting from the fingers in the center. Pin as you twist.*

2 *Tuck the ends in and secure with pins.*

3 *Bring up similar quantity of hair from the other side, wrap around the knot from behind and pin.*

4 *Wind the hair around the front of the knot and pin, tucking the ends beneath the knot.*

SHORT AND STRIKING

What you need
Water spray
Mousse
Hair dryer

Hair type
Short
Straight, Wavy, Curly

This is a great way of adding height and volume to short hair, a bold, challenging style that you can dress up with your brightest color combinations, like the Schiaparelli pink and peppermint green shown here.

You can style it like this after washing, or use a water spray to dampen it. Use a gentle heat to dry the hair — don't blast it with very hot air as this will tend to flatten it. Push your fingers through firmly, lift hair and hold for a few seconds each time. With most short styles, the hair on the sides of the head tends to be shorter, but pay attention to this as well to get a good, strong shape.

If your hair is totally straight, a quick application of heated shapers or a curling iron will give you the curl you need. Very curly hair, of course, will be a problem, as this kind of treatment just encourages it to go wild. Apply the waterspray liberally while you style and try not to use the dryer unless you absolutely must.

1 *Lightly dampen hair and apply mousse.*

2 *Begin to dry the hair, pushing your fingers through to lift the hair.*

3 *Use your fingers to shape the style.*

CURLY TOP

What you need
Covered elastic band
Hair pins
Hair spray

Hair type
Medium – Long
Straight, Wavy, Curly

Expensive hairdressers often use the most artificial means for the most natural results, which is why most people balk at the idea of creating an elaborate hair-do on their own. This style is unique in that it requires no accuracy or precision whatsoever: just make a ponytail, fluff up the ends and shove in some pins where you like. If your hair refuses to stay in a formal style, this is a brilliant alternative — why not capitalize on the chaos? The more untidy it is, the better it looks.

Straight hair can be curled with a curling iron after you've made the ponytail. Use plenty of hairspray to keep the curl. Whatever type of hair you have, spray is an essential ingredient. Keep a can in your evening bag for emergency repairs.

You can play up the fun and buoyancy with ribbons, bows or costume jewelry, make it soft and romantic with flowers — or just let it speak for itself.

1 *Make a loose ponytail on the crown of the head. Secure with elastic band.*

2 *Muss up your hair and tease it out (curl straight hair with curling iron).*

3 *Take a section of hair, lifting it with your hand and secure loosely with pins. Spray thoroughly.*

FRESH FLOWERS

What you need
Covered elastic band
Hair grips
Flowers or ornament

Hair type
Medium
Straight, Wavy

Clean, shining hair and fresh flowers are an irresistible combination. It is fairly simple to introduce a couple of flowers into a ready-made style, but when faced with an occasion like a wedding, when it is *de rigeur* to have several flowers and preferably some foliage as well, many people find it difficult to make the arrangement stay in place. This is a rapid solution.

Newly-washed hair is often slippery, so make sure the hair pins are firmly in place before you attach the flowers. The pins should overlap, forming a lattice pattern. Make sure your hair sits evenly where it is doubled over. If you find that there are overlapping, bulky bits, pull your hair apart and re-distribute it with a comb tail. The ends should splay out evenly, in a fan shape, balancing the doubled over hair at the bottom. If your hair could do with a trim, think twice about this style, as you may be putting split ends on display.

A row of individual flowers can be attached with pins, but it is easier to assemble a small spray before you start and bind the flowers together in the shape you want.

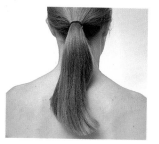

1 Secure hair just above the nape of the neck with a band.

2 Fold hair in half and pin, crossing pins over in a row. Fan the hair with your fingers and attach flowers.

MARCEL WAVE

What you need
Hair gel
Hairdresser's clips

Hair type
Short
Straight, Wavy

An updated version of an old idea, the Marcel wave has been with us for a very long time; in the twenties and early thirties, every woman had a rows of tight, elaborate waves which took forever to create. The style disappeared for a few decades but is now firmly back in fashion, and modern hair gel helps achieve a looser wave in minutes. The waves are actually formed between the side of a comb and your fingers, pushing together. With the hair gelled flat, these waves are only in one dimension. You don't have to worry about body or a good shape (often the most difficult thing to achieve styling short hair) because the style is the shape of your head. The secret of a perfect Marcel wave is to leave the clips in place until the gel has set. Concentrate on your make-up and clothes and take the clips out just before you leave home.

This style is sensational with a backless evening dress, a ball gown or a simple silk blouse.

1 *Apply gel. Part and comb your hair.*

2 *Push the hair into waves between a comb and your fingers.*

3 *Secure waves with hairdresser's clips.*

THE BEEHIVE

What you need
Hairdresser's clips
Hair pins
Hairspray

Hair type
Medium – Long
Straight, Wavy, Curly

Taken to excess, this style can be a top-heavy lump of dull, tangled hair, but a restrained beehive is stylish and extremely flattering. Small, delicate accessories won't do much for this look: try jet or diamanté earrings or a big, bright bow pinned on the back for an instant party look.

The mainstay of a beehive is the small French roll at the back of the head. You can backcomb the remaining hair as much or as little as you like depending on how much height you want. This is where hairspray comes into its own — to ensure that your hair stays firmly in place, spray as you backcomb. When you bring all the sections of backcombed hair together, make sure that the front hair is smooth, with no snarls or lumps. Needlesss to say, it is advisable to brush your hair out properly at night.

1 Divide front and back hair, clip the front hair out of the way while you make a French roll (see page 8).

2 Backcomb hair in sections, starting at front hairline and working backwards.

3 Bring all the backcombed hair together in one strand. Bend the top over your hand and fold it over the roll. Pin in place.

EDWARDIAN ELEGANCE

What you need
Hair pins

Hair type
Long
Straight, Wavy, Curly

If your hair curls naturally, it is a shame to bundle it all up on top of your head and hide it. This is a good way of wearing your hair up without obscuring the curls. This lovely look suits all ages and face shapes and is a great way to soften a severe shirt collar and cravat or compliment a frilly neckline and a cameo pin.

It is also suitable for straight hair, although it isn't possible to achieve the wispy curls at the front. Instead, keep the front very smooth and have a couple of larger 'sausage' type curls on the forehead.

Your hair needs to be long enough to make the topknot; hair which is only a couple of inches below the shoulders is really too short to make a good-sized knot so high on the head, as the style needs the loose effect at the front.

1 *Gather your hair into a ponytail and bring it up to crown. Hold the ponytail with one hand. Wrap the end of it around the other.*

2 *Pull the hair through as if knotting.*

3 *When hair is pulled right through, tuck the ends into the middle and secure with pins.*

RINGLETS AND ROSES

What you need
Barette or slide
Flowers or ornament
Mousse

Hair type
Long
Straight, Wavy, Curly

A little black dress is the perfect accompaniment for this style, with its strong hint of old fashioned nightclubs and smoky, jazz-filled rooms. Billie Holliday favored gardenias in her hair, but small white roses or carnations are fine for this sultry look. There are many other ways to wear this style: add a high tortoiseshell comb draped with lace for a Spanish effect, or try it with fake fruit and a sarong.

You can do this style with straight hair, omitting the mousse. If you want to have curls, use heated shapers — but be warned, they will have to be in your hair for some time to achieve this effect (it may be better to curl the hair overnight in curlers or rags). Do not use mousse afterwards, as this will tend to remove the curl.

Do not pull your hair up too tightly at the side, as curly hair tends to form unsightly bumps and straight hair which is pulled upwards can look very harsh.

1 *Lift up hair on one side, smoothing with comb.*

2 *Slide barette into this section of hair and secure it across the head.*

3 *Scrunch mousse into hair. Add decoration of your choice.*

SIMPLE CHIGNON VARIATION

What you need
Covered elastic band
Hair pins
Hair comb

Hair Type
Medium – Long
Straight, Wavy, Curly

This is an instant way of converting a daytime style (page 56) into a dramatic evening look. You need a distinctive comb, with a high top and long, wide teeth. This Spanish comb is ideal, because it holds the hair securely in place and provides a beautiful decoration at the same time. If you find a comb with long teeth which is unremarkable or rather elderly you can rejuvinate it by gluing on a few silk flowers or a piece of brocade ribbon.

You don't need to take much hair from the chignon — pull it towards your head gently with your finger and thumb. If it feels as if it is attached to a pin underneath the chignon, extract it carefully, loosen the hair and replace the pin. Push back any strands of hair that have escaped from the chignon in the process. You can use hairspray for extra security.

1 *Remove ribbon. Take the hair from both sides of the chignon and pull it gently upwards, pinching it together.*

2 *Push the teeth of a large comb in between chignon and back of head to hold it upright.*

ROMANTIC CHIGNON

What you need
Hair pins
Hair grips
Hair ornament

Hair type
Long
Straight, Wavy, Curly

This is a variation on the classic chignon, much favored by Victorian ladies for its demure, feminine look. They knew that it was a practical, as well as an elegant way to show off long, thick hair; there is nothing worse than spending an evening with a top-heavy pile of hair precariously perched on your head, afraid to move in case it topples over.

The chignon can be a sophisticated style, perfect for a backless evening dress and glittering accessories. Soft flattering curves frame the face and neck beautifully.

Smoothing the front hair with a comb as you pin it up will ensure a good, firm shape. Keep a few pins handy to secure any stray locks of hair. If the back does collapse on you, it is easy to resurrect — just twist it up tightly and poke in a few discreet pins. An ornament pinned at the center of the chignon will help to hide them.

1 Draw hair back from the side of the head twisting upwards to make a soft roll, pinning as you go. Repeat on the other side.

2 Smooth the rolls of hair with a comb. Secure the two rolls of hair together at the back of the head.

3 Divide remaining hair into two equal sections. Twist each section into a corkscrew. Bring corkscrew up to crown in a loop, pin ends.

4 Repeat process on the other side. Pin the insides of the loops together in the middle. Fluff out the tufts of hair in the center.

FRENCH ROLL VARIATION

What you need
Hair wax

Hair type
Medium – Long
Straight, Wavy

This is a witty transformation for a hairstyle that takes itself very seriously. Your hair retains its elegant up-sweep at the back, and the bubbly curls fountaining outwards in a topknot make a charming style for a party. Give your most dignified evening gown a touch of frivolity.

Be very careful when loosening the top of the roll. A well made roll will keep its shape, but if any of the pins have slipped, the hair may collapse on you. Free the ends of the hair gently; if you try to pull out a whole bunch at once, it will certainly fall down. If the roll feels precarious, shore it up with a few extra pins. You can always remove them afterwards.

If your hair is very straight, you will need to give the ends a gentle curl with the tongs. Otherwise, curl them around your fingers with a bit of wax to keep the hair smooth.

1 Loosen the top of the French roll slightly (see page 58) and untuck the ends of the hair.

2 Secure the top of the roll with pins.

3 Backcomb the loose ends and form a top knot by separating the hair into fluffy loose curls.

INDEX